Impressum
Verlag: BABADADA GmbH, Nedderfeld 112 , 22529 Hamburg
Geschäftsführer / Verlagsleitung: Harald Hof
Druck: Books on Demand GmbH, In de Tarpen 42, 22848 Norderstedt

Imprint
Publisher: BABADADA GmbH, Nedderfeld 112 , 22529 Hamburg, Germany
Managing Director / Publishing direction: Harald Hof
Print: Books on Demand GmbH, In de Tarpen 42, 22848 Norderstedt

escuela

school

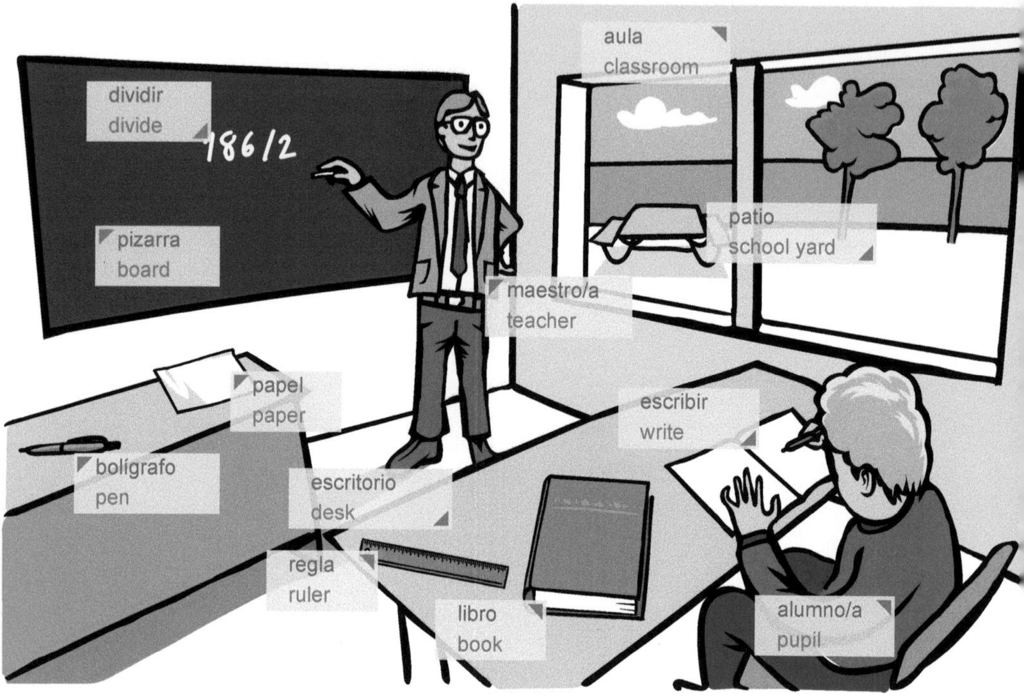

aula
classroom
dividir
divide
186/2
pizarra
board
patio
school yard
maestro/a
teacher
papel
paper
escribir
write
bolígrafo
pen
escritorio
desk
regla
ruler
libro
book
alumno/a
pupil

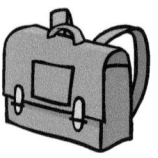

cartera

satchel

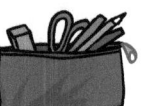

caja de lápices

pencil case

lápiz

pencil

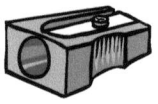

sacapuntas

pencil sharpener

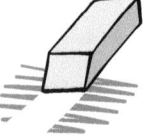

goma de borrar

rubber

cuaderno de dibujo

drawing pad

dibujo

drawing

pincel

paintbrush

caja de pinturas

paint box

tijeras

scissors

pegamento

glue

cuaderno de ejercicios

exercise book

deberes

homework

número

number

2+2

sumar

add

5-2

restar

subtract

2×2

multiplicar

multiply

calcular

calculate

A

letra

letter

ABCDEFG
HIJKLMN
OPQRSTU
VWXYZ

alfabeto

alphabet

palabra

word

texto

text

leer

read

tiza

chalk

lección

lesson

cuaderno de notas

register

examen

examination

certificado

certificate

uniforme escolar

school uniform

educación

education

enciclopedia

encyclopedia

universidad

university

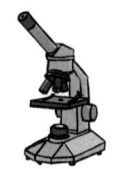

microscopio

microscope

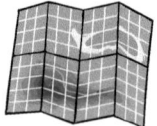

mapa

map

papelera

waste-paper basket

hotel
hotel

Grand

albergue
hostel

ROOMS

oficina de cambio de divisas
currency exchange office

EXCHANGE

maleta
suitcase

coche
car

idioma
language

sí / no
yes / no

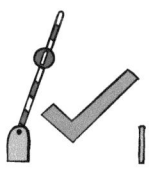

Vale
Okay

hola
hello

traductor
translator

Gracias
Thank you

¿cuánto es...?

how much is...?

No entiendo

I don't get it

problema

problem

¡Buenas tardes!

Good evening!

¡Buenos días!

Good morning!

¡Buenas noches!

Good night!

adiós

goodbye

dirección

direction

equipaje

luggage

bolsa

bag

mochila

backpack

invitado

guest

habitación

room

saco de dormir

sleeping bag

tienda de campaña

tent

información turística

tourist information

playa

beach

tarjeta de crédito

credit card

desayuno

breakfast

almuerzo

lunch

cena

dinner

billete

Ticket

ascensor

elevator

sello

stamp

frontera

border

aduana

customs

embajada

embassy

visa

visa

pasaporte

passport

viaje - travel

transporte
transport

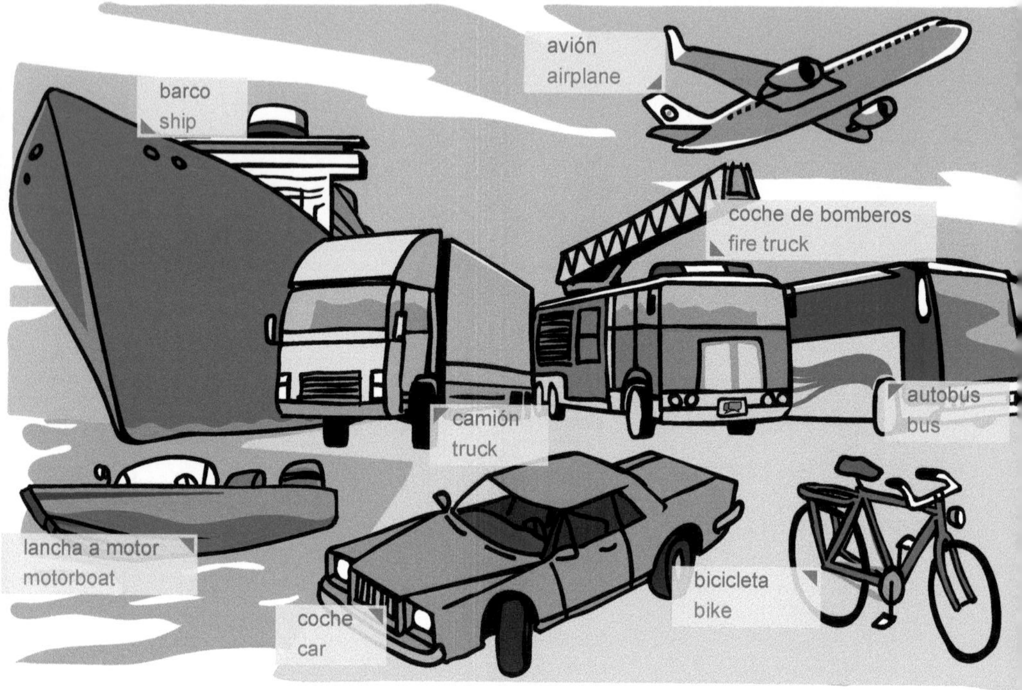
avión
airplane
barco
ship
coche de bomberos
fire truck
autobús
bus
camión
truck
lancha a motor
motorboat
bicicleta
bike
coche
car

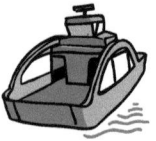

transbordador

ferry

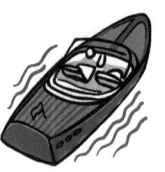

barca

boat

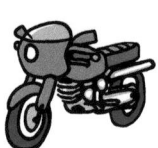

moto

motorbike

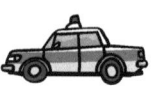

coche de policía

police car

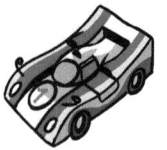

coche de carreras

racing car

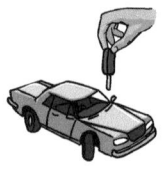

coche de alquiler

rental car

préstamo de vehículos

car sharing

grúa

tow truck

camión de la basura

garbage truck

motor

engine

gasolina

fuel

gasolinera

fuel station

señal de tráfico

traffic sign

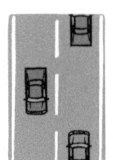

tráfico

traffic

atasco

traffic jam

aparcamiento

parking lot

estación de tren

train station

vías

tracks

tren

train

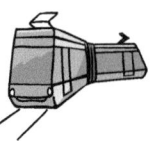

tranvía

tram

vagón

wagon

helicóptero
helicopter

aeropuerto
airport

torre
tower

pasajero
passenger

contenedor
container

caja de cartón
carton

carretilla
cart

cesta
basket

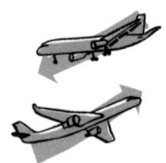

despegar / aterrizar
take off / land

ciudad
city

pueblo
village

centro de ciudad
city center

casa
house

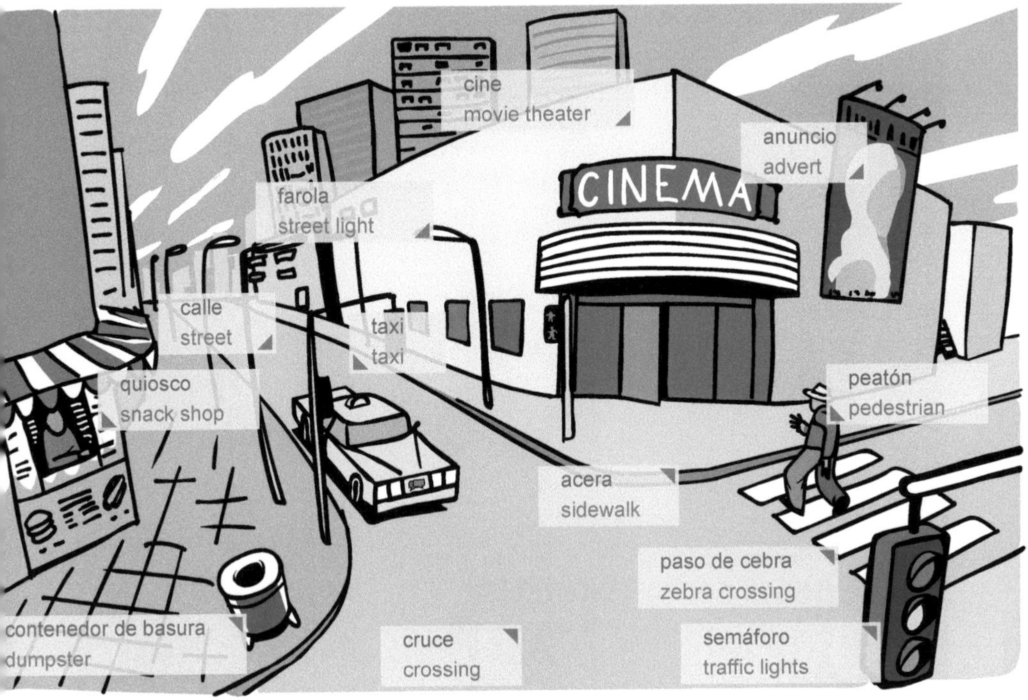

cine
movie theater

anuncio
advert

farola
street light

calle
street

taxi
taxi

quiosco
snack shop

CINEMA

peatón
pedestrian

acera
sidewalk

paso de cebra
zebra crossing

contenedor de basura
dumpster

cruce
crossing

semáforo
traffic lights

cabaña
hut

apartamento
apartment

estación de tren
train station

ayuntamiento
city hall

museo
museum

escuela
school

ciudad - city

universidad

university

banco

bank

hospital

hospital

hotel

hotel

farmacia

pharmacy

oficina

office

librería

book shop

tienda

shop

floristería

flower shop

supermercado

supermarket

mercado

market

grandes almacenes

department store

pescadería

fishmonger's shop

centro comercial

mall

puerto

harbor

parque
park

banco
bench

puente
bridge

escaleras
stairs

metro
subway

túnel
tunnel

parada de autobús
bus stop

bar
bar

restaurante
restaurant

buzón
postbox

poste indicador
street sign

parquímetro
parking meter

zoo
zoo

piscina
swimming pool

mezquita
mosque

granja

farm

contaminación

pollution

cementerio

cemetery

iglesia

church

patio de juego

playground

templo

temple

paisaje
landscape

hoja
leaf

señal
signpost

camino
path

prado
meadow

piedra
stone

excursionista
hiker

árbol
tree

río
river

hierba
grass

flor
flower

valle
valley

colina
hill

lago
lake

bosque
forest

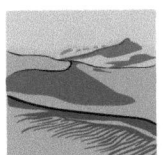

desierto
desert

volcán
volcano

castillo
castle

arcoíris
rainbow

champiñón
mushroom

palmera
palm tree

mosquito
mosquito

mosca
fly

hormiga
ant

abeja
bee

araña
spider

escarabajo

beetle

rana

frog

ardilla

squirrel

erizo

hedgehog

liebre

hare

lechuza

owl

pájaro

bird

cisne

swan

jabalí

boar

ciervo

deer

alce

moose

presa

dam

turbina eólica

wind turbine

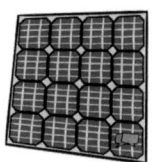

panel solar

solar panel

clima

climate

camarero
waiter

menú
menu

silla
chair

sopa
soup

pizza
pizza

cubertería
cutlery

mantel
tablecloth

primer plato
starter

plato principal
main course

postre
dessert

bebidas
drinks

comida
food

botella
bottle

comida rápida

fast food

comida callejera

street food

tetera

teapot

azucarero

sugar bowl

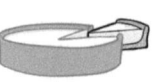

porción

portion

cafetera expreso

espresso machine

trona

high chair

cuenta

bill

bandeja

tray

cuchillo

knife

tenedor

fork

cuchara

spoon

cucharilla

teaspoon

servilleta

serviette

vaso

glass

plato
plate

plato hondo
soup plate

platillo
saucer

salsa
sauce

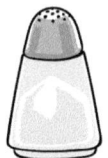

salero
salt shaker

molinillo de pimienta
pepper mill

vinagre
vinegar

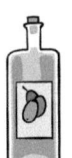

aceite
oil

especias
spices

ketchup
ketchup

mostaza
mustard

mayonesa
mayonnaise

supermercado
supermarket

oferta especial
special offer
FOR
cliente
customer
lácteos
dairy products
fruta
fruit
carro de la compra
shopping cart

BUTCHERS

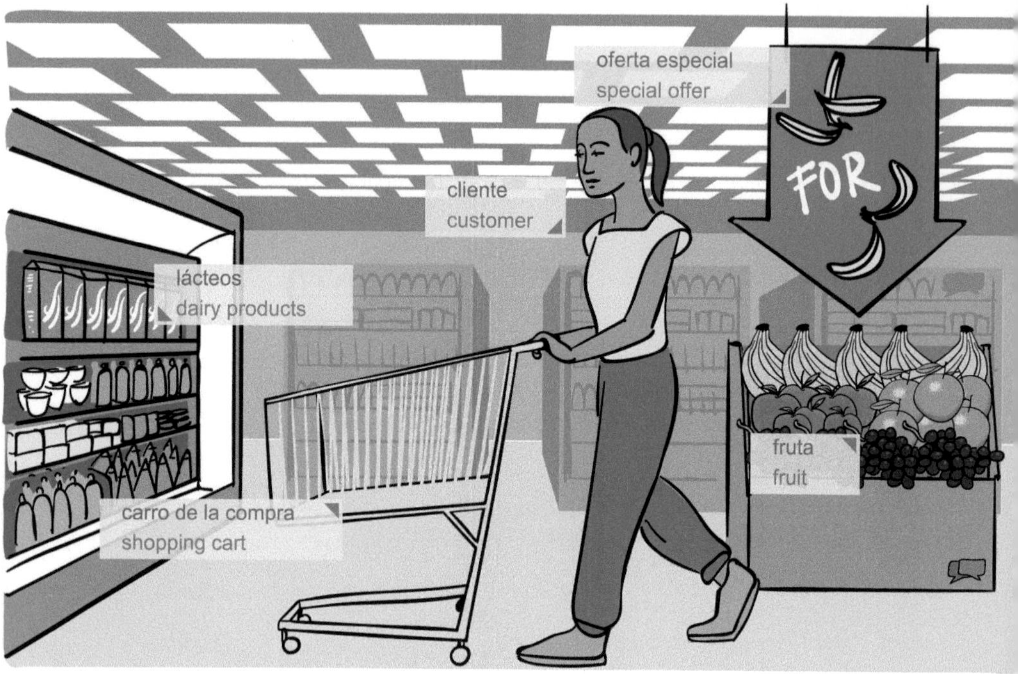

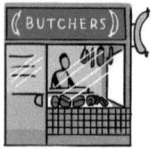

carnicería

butcher's shop

BAKERY

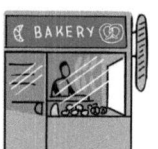

panadería

bakery

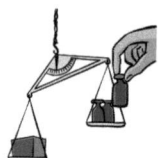

pesar

weigh

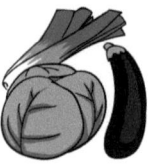

verduras

vegetables

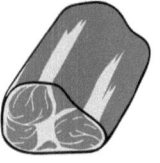

carne

meat

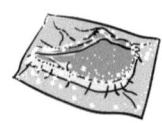

alimentos congelados

frozen food

fiambres

cold cuts

conservas

canned food

detergente en polvo

detergent

dulces

candy

productos de uso doméstico

household products

productos de limpieza

cleaning products

vendedora

sales representative

caja

cash register

cajero

cashier

lista de la compra

shopping list

horario de atención al público

opening hours

cartera

wallet

tarjeta de crédito

credit card

bolsa

bag

bolsa de plástico

plastic bag

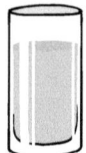

agua

water

zumo

juice

leche

milk

cola

coke

vino

wine

cerveza

beer

alcohol

alcohol

cacao

cocoa

té

tea

café

coffee

expreso

espresso

capuchino

cappuccino

plátano

banana

manzana

apple

naranja

orange

melón

melon

limón

lemon

zanahoria

carrot

ajo

garlic

bambú

bamboo

cebolla

onion

champiñón

mushroom

avellanas

nuts

fideos

noodles

espagueti

spaghetti

arroz

rice

ensalada

salad

patatas fritas

fries

patatas fritas

fried potatoes

pizza

pizza

hamburguesa

hamburger

sándwich

sandwich

filete

escalope

jamón

ham

salami

salami

salchicha

sausage

pollo

chicken

asado

roast

pescado

fish

comida - food

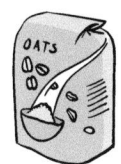

copos de avena

porridge oats

muesli

muesli

copos de maíz

cornflakes

harina

flour

cruasán

croissant

panecillo

bread roll

pan

bread

tostada

toast

galletas

cookies

mantequilla

butter

cuajada

curd

pastel

cake

huevo

egg

huevo frito

fried egg

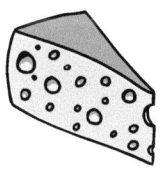

queso

cheese

helado

ice cream

azúcar

sugar

miel

honey

mermelada

jelly

crema de turrón

nougat cream

curry

curry

granja
farm

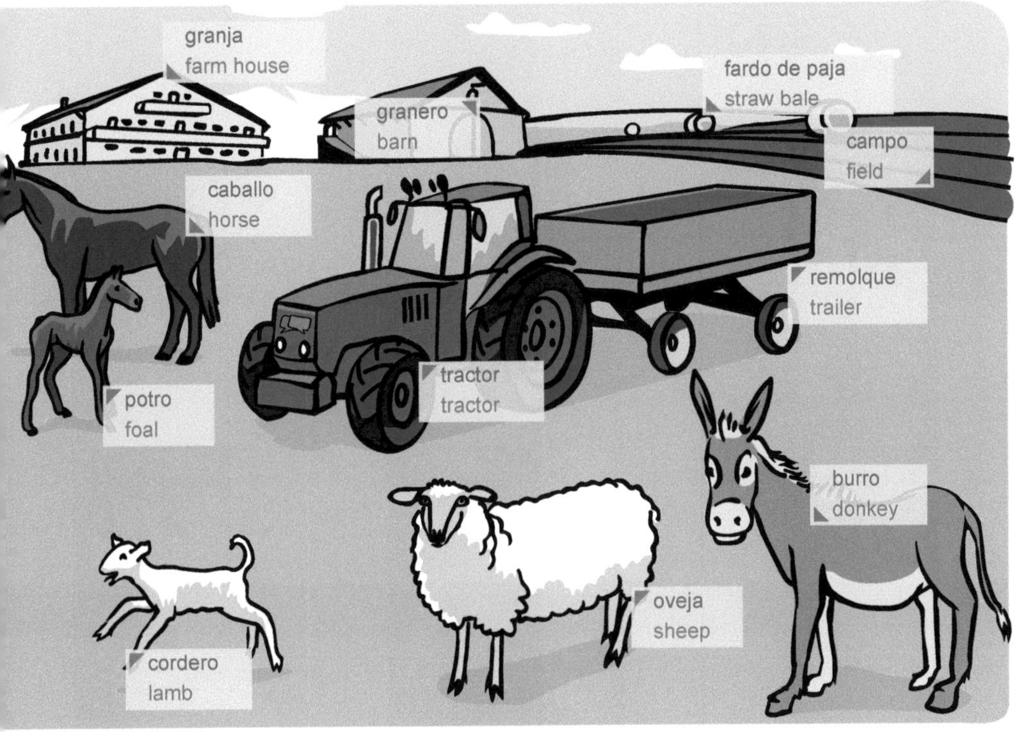
granja
farm house
granero
barn
fardo de paja
straw bale
campo
field
caballo
horse
remolque
trailer
tractor
tractor
potro
foal
burro
donkey
oveja
sheep
cordero
lamb

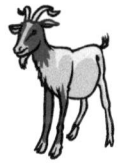

cabra

goat

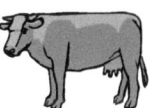

vaca

cow

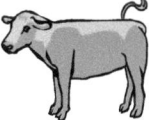

ternero

calf

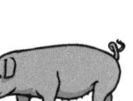

cerdo

pig

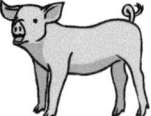

cerdito

piglet

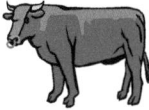

toro

bull

ganso

goose

pato

duck

pollo

chick

gallina

hen

gallo

cockerel

rata

rat

gato

cat

ratón

mouse

buey

ox

perro

dog

perrera

dog house

manguera

garden hose

regadera

watering can

guadaña

scythe

arado

plow

hoz

sickle

azada

hoe

horca

pitchfork

hacha

axe

carretilla

pushcart

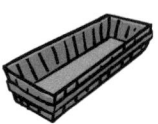

abrevadero

trough

lechera

milk can

saco

sack

valla

fence

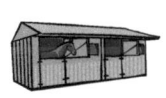

establo

stable

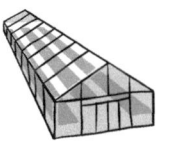

invernadero

greenhouse

suelo

soil

semilla

seed

fertilizador

fertilizer

cosechadora

combine harvester

cosechar

harvest

cosecha

harvest

ñame

yams

trigo

wheat

soja

soya

patata

potato

maíz

corn

semilla de colza

rapeseed

árbol frutal

fruit tree

mandioca

manioc

cereales

grain

casa
house

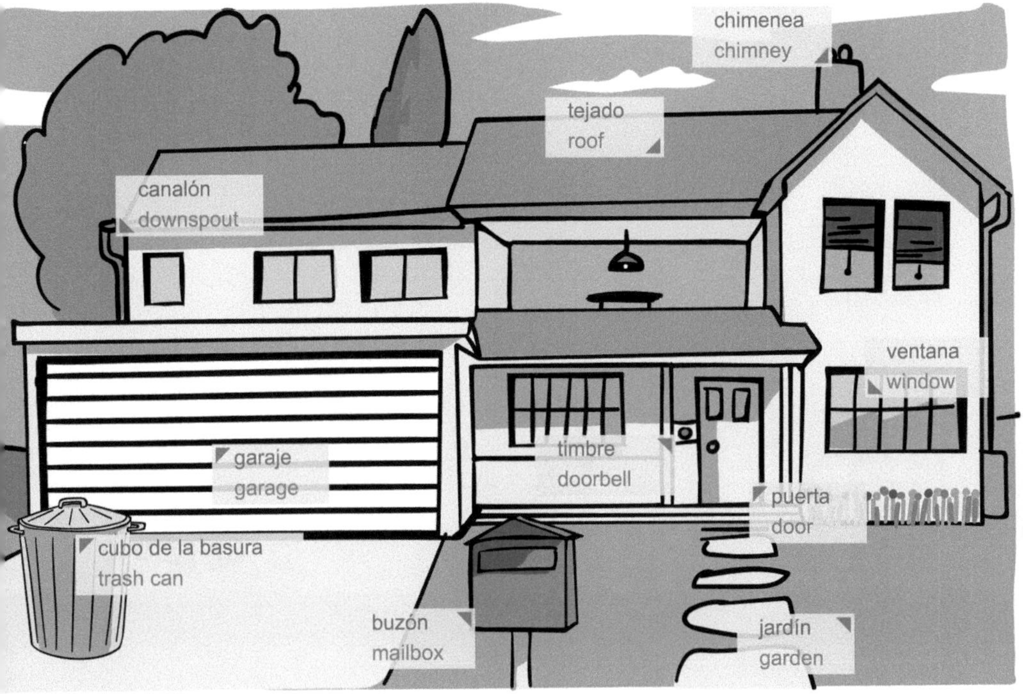
chimenea
chimney
tejado
roof
canalón
downspout
ventana
window
timbre
doorbell
garaje
garage
puerta
door
cubo de la basura
trash can
buzón
mailbox
jardín
garden

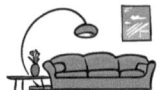

sala

living room

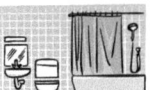

cuarto de baño

bathroom

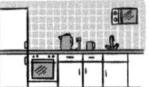

cocina

kitchen

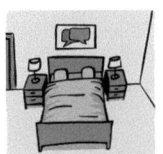

dormitorio

bedroom

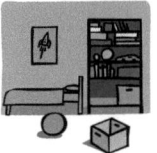

habitación de los niños

kids room

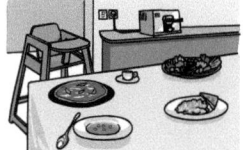

comedor

dining room

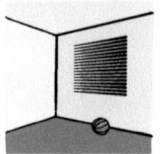

suelo
floor

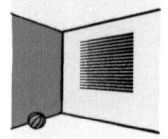

pared
wall

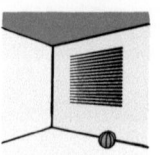

techo
ceiling

sótano
cellar

sauna
sauna

balcón
balcony

terraza
terrace

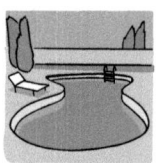

piscina
pool

cortacésped
lawn mower

sábana
sheet

colcha
bedspread

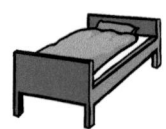

cama
bed

escoba
broom

balde
bucket

interruptor
switch

sala

living room

papel pintado
wallpaper
imagen
picture
lámpara
lamp
estante
shelf
armario
cabinet
televisión
television
chimenea
fireplace
flor
flower
cojín
cushion
sofá
sofa
jarrón
vase
mando a distancia
remote control

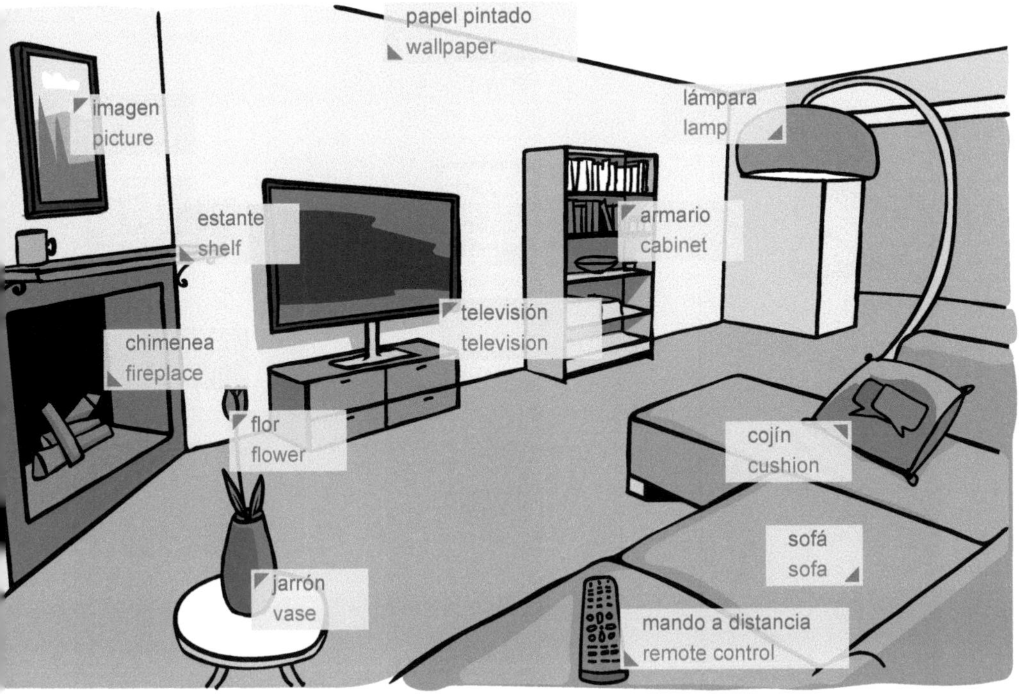

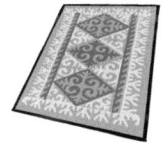

alfombra

carpet

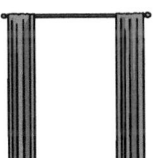

cortina

drape

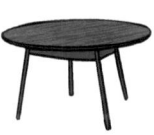

mesa

table

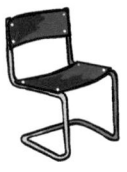

silla

chair

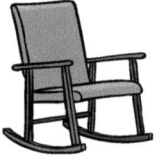

mecedora

rocking chair

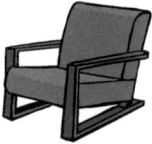

butaca

armchair

libro
book

manta
blanket

decoración
decoration

leña
firewood

película
film

equipo de música
stereo system

llave
key

periódico
newspaper

pintura
painting

póster
poster

radio
radio

cuaderno
notebook

aspiradora
vacuum cleaner

cactus
cactus

vela
candle

cocina
kitchen

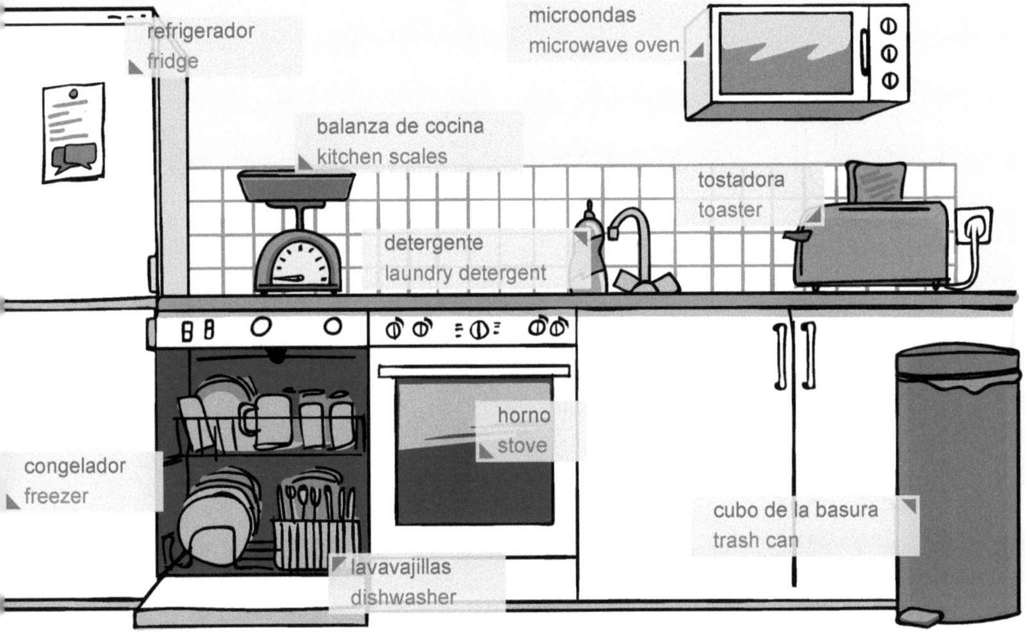
refrigerador
fridge
microondas
microwave oven
balanza de cocina
kitchen scales
tostadora
toaster
detergente
laundry detergent
horno
stove
congelador
freezer
cubo de la basura
trash can
lavavajillas
dishwasher

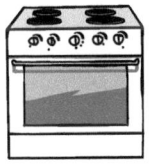

olla a presión

cooker

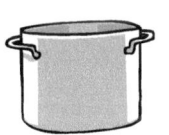

olla

pot

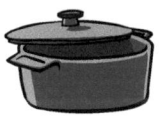

olla de hierro fundido

cast-iron pot

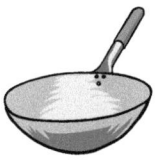

wok / karahi

wok / kadai

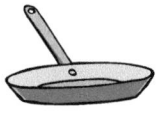

cazuela

pan

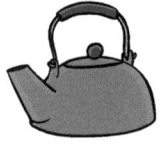

hervidor

kettle

vaporera

steamer

chapa de horno

baking tray

vajilla

crockery

taza

mug

tazón

bowl

palillos

chopsticks

cucharón

ladle

espumadera

spatula

batidor

whisk

colador

strainer

cedazo

sieve

rallador

grater

mortero

mortar

barbacoa

barbecue

hoguera

fireplace

tabla de picar

chopping board

rodillo

rolling pin

sacacorchos

corkscrew

lata

can

abrelatas

can opener

agarrador

oven cloth

lavabo

sink

cepillo

brush

esponja

sponge

batidora

blender

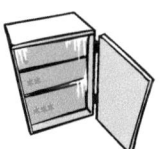

congelador

deep freezer

biberón

baby bottle

grifo

tap

cuarto de baño
bathroom

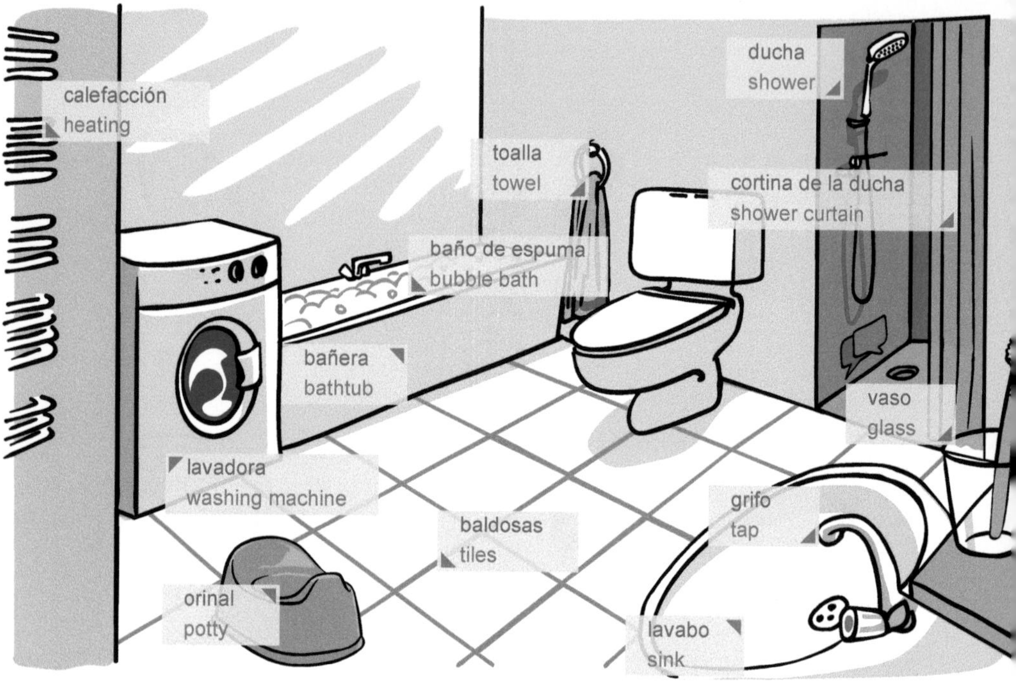
ducha
shower
calefacción
heating
toalla
towel
cortina de la ducha
shower curtain
baño de espuma
bubble bath
bañera
bathtub
vaso
glass
lavadora
washing machine
grifo
tap
baldosas
tiles
orinal
potty
lavabo
sink

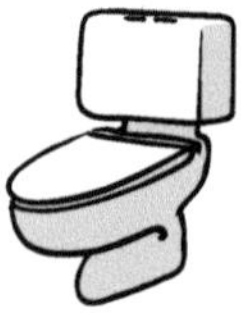

inodoro

toilet

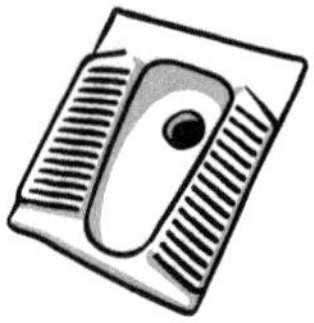

inodoro rústico

squat toilet

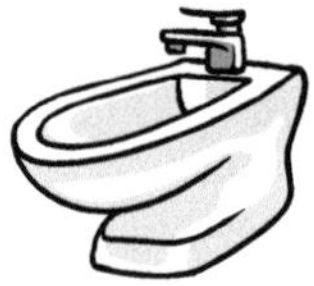

bidé

bidet

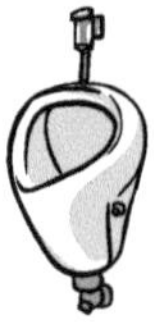

urinario

urinal

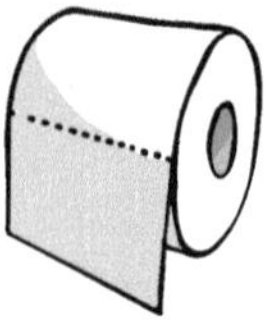

papel higiénico

toilet paper

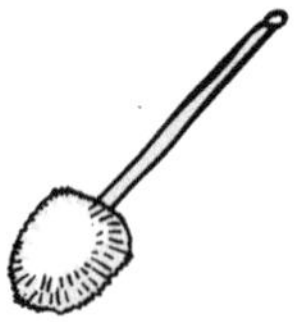

escobilla del váter

toilet brush

cepillo de dientes

toothbrush

pasta de dientes

toothpaste

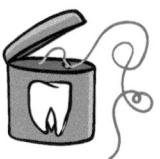

hilo dental

dental floss

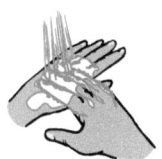

lavar

wash

ducha de mano

hand shower

ducha íntima

douche

pila

basin

cepillo de espalda

back brush

jabón

soap

gel de ducha

shower gel

champú

shampoo

toallita

flannel

desagüe

drain

crema

creme

desodorante

deodorant

cuarto de baño - bathroom

espejo

mirror

espejo de tocador

hand mirror

maquinilla de afeitar

razor

espuma de afeitar

shaving foam

loción postafeitado

aftershave

peine

comb

cepillo

brush

secador

hair-dryer

laca

hairspray

maquillaje

makeup

pintalabios

lipstick

pintauñas

nail varnish

algodón

cotton wool

cortauñas

nail scissors

perfume

perfume

estuche de viaje

washbag

banqueta

stool

balanza

weighing scales

albornoz

bathrobe

guantes de goma

rubber gloves

tampón

tampon

compresa

sanitary towel

inodoro químico

chemical toilet

habitación de los niños

kids room

despertador
alarm clock
peluche
cuddly toy
coche de juguete
toy car
sonajero
rattle
casa de muñecas
doll's house
regalo
present

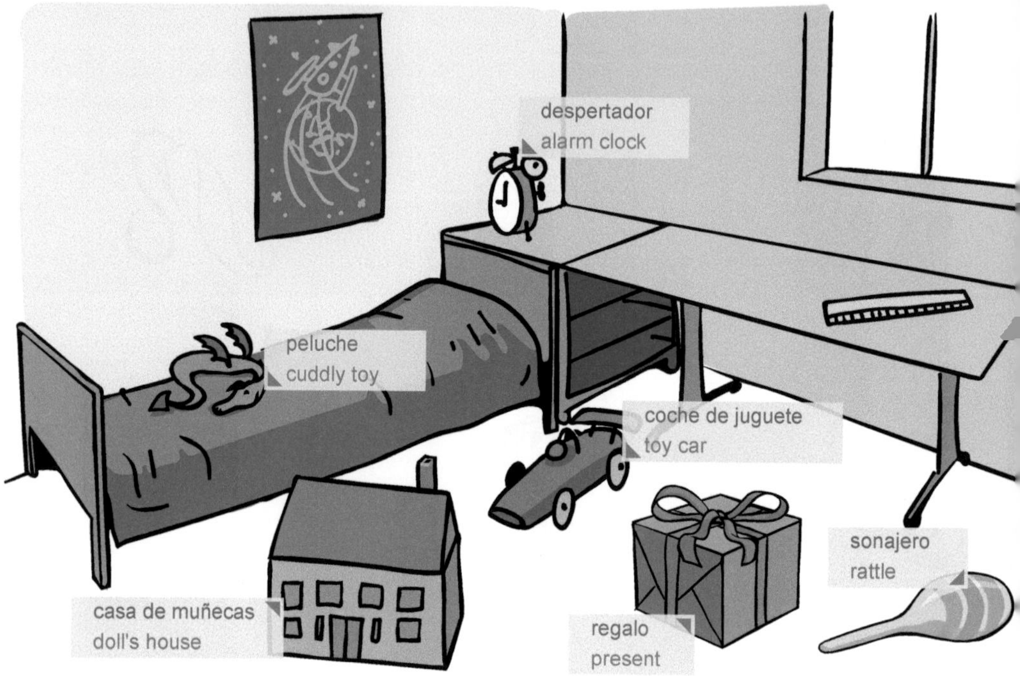

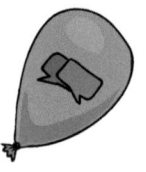

globo

balloon

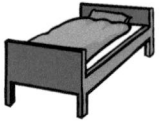

cama

bed

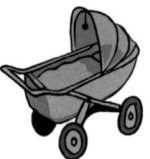

coche de niño

stroller

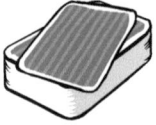

naipes

deck of cards

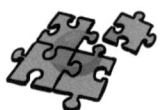

puzle

jigsaw

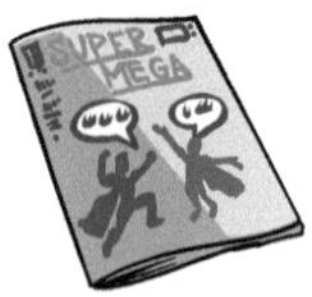

tebeo

comic

piezas de lego

lego bricks

bloques de juguete

toy blocks

figura de acción

action figure

bodi (de bebé)

romper suit

frisbee

frisbee

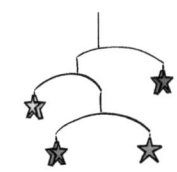

colgador móvil para bebés

mobile

juego de mesa

board game

dados

dice

circuito de tren eléctrico

model train set

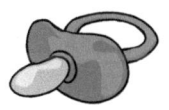

maniquí

pacifier

fiesta

party

álbum de fotos

picture book

pelota

ball

muñeca

doll

jugar

play

cajón de arena

sandpit

columpio

swing

juguetes

toys

videoconsola

video game console

triciclo

tricycle

oso de peluche

teddy bear

guardarropa

wardrobe

ropa
clothing

calcetines

socks

medias

stockings

leotardos

tights

bufanda
scarf

paraguas
umbrella

camiseta
t-shirt

cinturón
belt

zapatillas
slippers

botas
boots

deportivas
sneakers

sandalias	zapatos	botas de goma
sandals	shoes	rubber boots
slip	sostén	chaleco
underwear	bra	undershirt

ropa - clothing

bodi
body

pantalones
pants

vaqueros
jeans

falda
skirt

blusa
blouse

camisa
shirt

jersey
pullover

suéter
sweater

blazer
blazer

chaqueta
jacket

abrigo
coat

gabardina
raincoat

traje
costume

vestido
dress

vestido de novia
wedding dress

traje
suit

camisón
nightgown

pijama
pajamas

sari
sari

bandana
headscarf

turbante
turban

burka
burka

caftán
kaftan

abaya
abaya

traje de baño
swimsuit

bañador
trunks

pantalones cortos
shorts

chándal
tracksuit

delantal
apron

guantes
gloves

botón

button

gafas

glasses

brazalete

bracelet

collar

necklace

anillo

ring

pendiente

earring

gorra

cap

percha

coat hanger

sombrero

hat

corbata

tie

cremallera

zip

casco

helmet

tirantes

braces

uniforme escolar

school uniform

uniforme

uniform

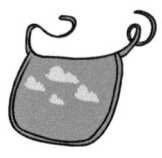

babero

bib

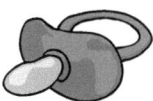

maniquí

pacifier

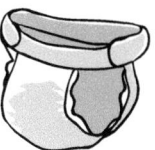

pañal

diaper

oficina

office

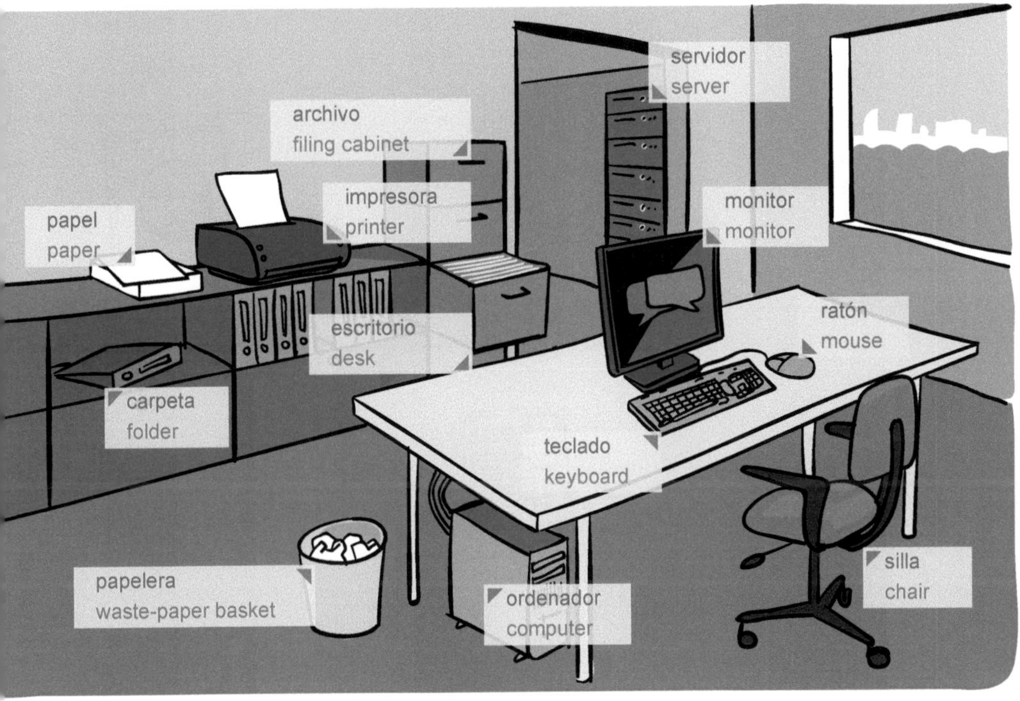
servidor
server
archivo
filing cabinet
impresora
printer
papel
paper
monitor
monitor
ratón
mouse
escritorio
desk
carpeta
folder
teclado
keyboard
papelera
waste-paper basket
ordenador
computer
silla
chair

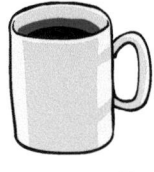

taza de café

coffee mug

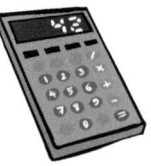

calculadora

calculator

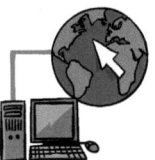

internet

internet

portátil

laptop

carta

letter

mensaje

message

móvil

cell phone

red

network

fotocopiadora

photocopier

software

software

teléfono

telephone

toma de corriente

plug socket

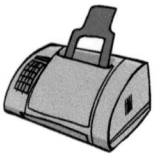

fax

fax machine

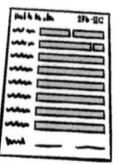

formulario

form

documento

document

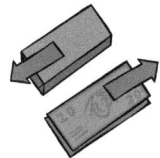

comprar
buy

pagar
pay

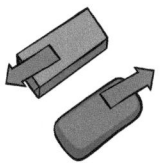

comerciar
trade

dinero
money

USD

dólar
dollar

EUR

euro
euro

JPY

yen
yen

RUB

rublo
rouble

CHF

franco suizo
Swiss franc

CNY

renminbi yuan
renminbi yuan

INR

rupia
rupee

cajero automático
cash point

oficina de cambio de divisas

currency exchange office

oro

gold

plata

silver

petróleo

oil

energía

energy

precio

price

contrato

contract

impuesto

tax

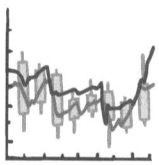

acción

stock

trabajar

work

empleado

employee

empleador

employer

fábrica

factory

tienda

shop

oficios
occupations

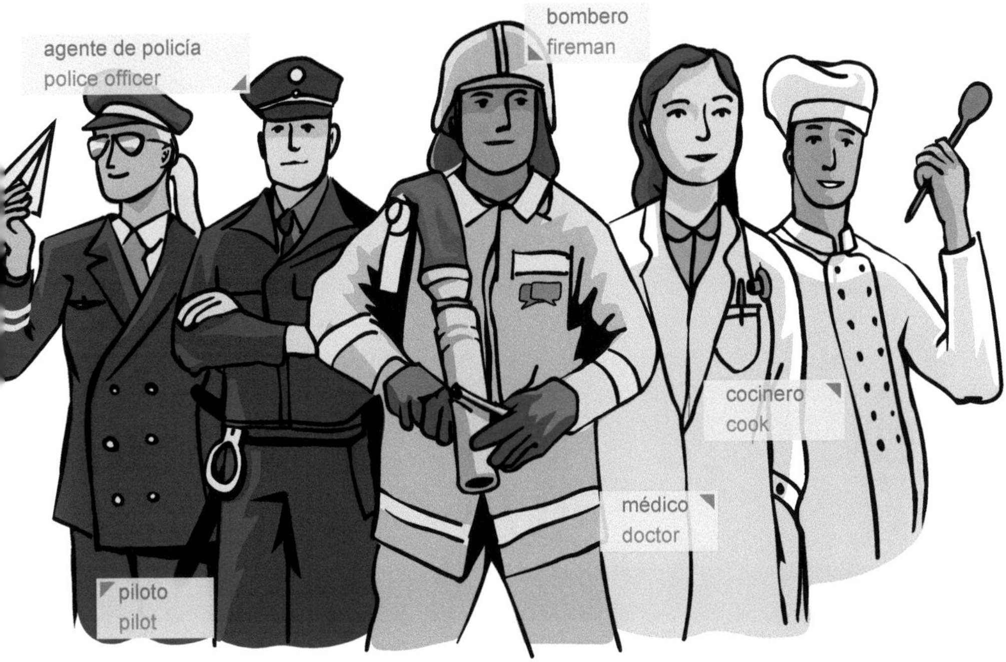
agente de policía
police officer
bombero
fireman
cocinero
cook
médico
doctor
piloto
pilot

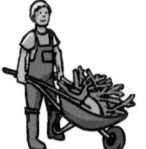

jardinero

gardener

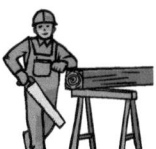

carpintero

carpenter

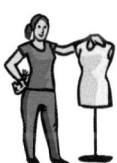

costurera

seamstress

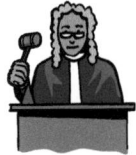

juez

judge

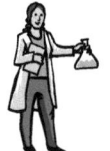

farmacéutico

chemist

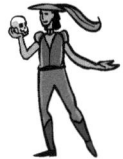

actor

actor

conductor de autobús

bus driver

taxista

taxi driver

pescador

fisherman

señora de la limpieza

cleaning lady

techador

roofer

camarero

waiter

cazador

hunter

pintor

painter

panadero

baker

electricista

electrician

obrero

builder

ingeniero

engineer

carnicero

butcher

fontanero

plumber

cartero

postman

oficios - occupations

soldado
soldier

arquitecto
architect

cajero
cashier

florista
florist

peluquero
hairdresser

revisor
conductor

mecánico
mechanic

capitán
captain

dentista
dentist

científico
scientist

rabino
rabbi

imán
imam

monje
monk

sacerdote
pastor

herramientas
tools

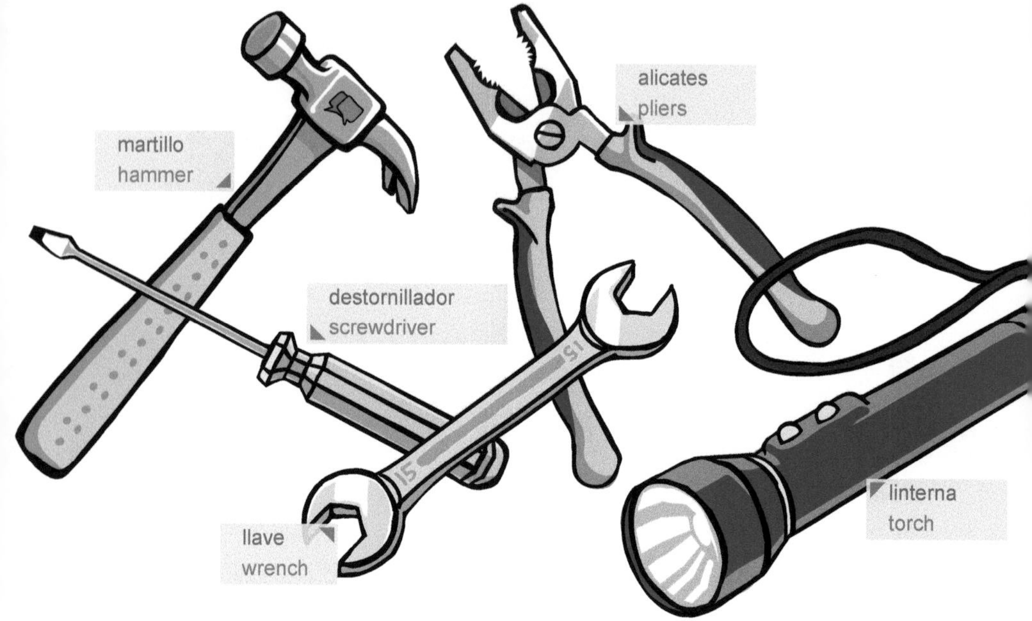
martillo
hammer
alicates
pliers
destornillador
screwdriver
llave
wrench
linterna
torch

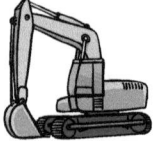

excavadora

excavator

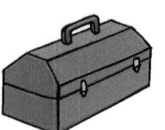

caja de herramientas

toolbox

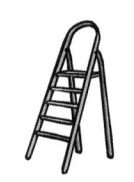

escalera de mano

ladder

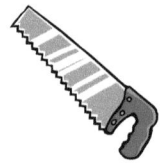

sierra

saw

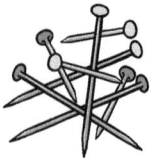

clavos

nails

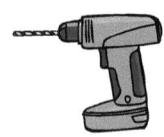

taladro

drill

reparar
repair

pala
shovel

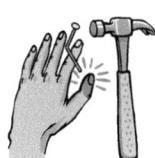

¡Maldita sea!
Damn!

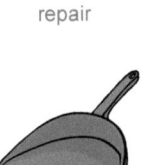

recogedor
dustpan

bote de pintura
paint can

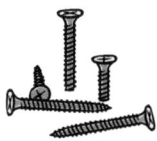

tornillos
screws

instrumentos musicales
musical instruments

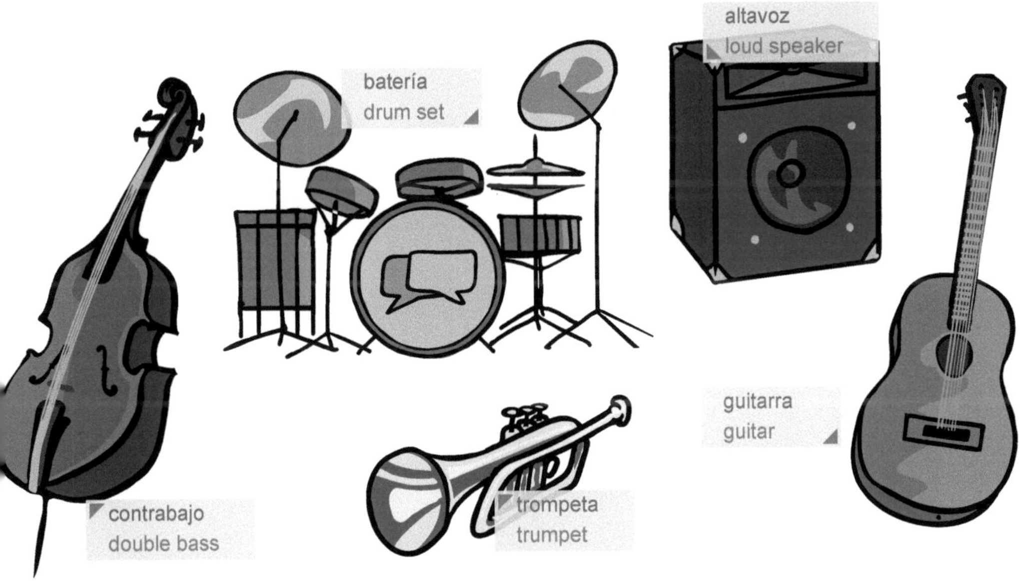

batería
drum set

altavoz
loud speaker

guitarra
guitar

contrabajo
double bass

trompeta
trumpet

piano	violín	bajo
piano	violin	bass

timbales	tambor	teclado
timpani	drums	keyboard

saxofón	flauta	micrófono
saxophone	flute	microphone

instrumentos musicales - musical instruments

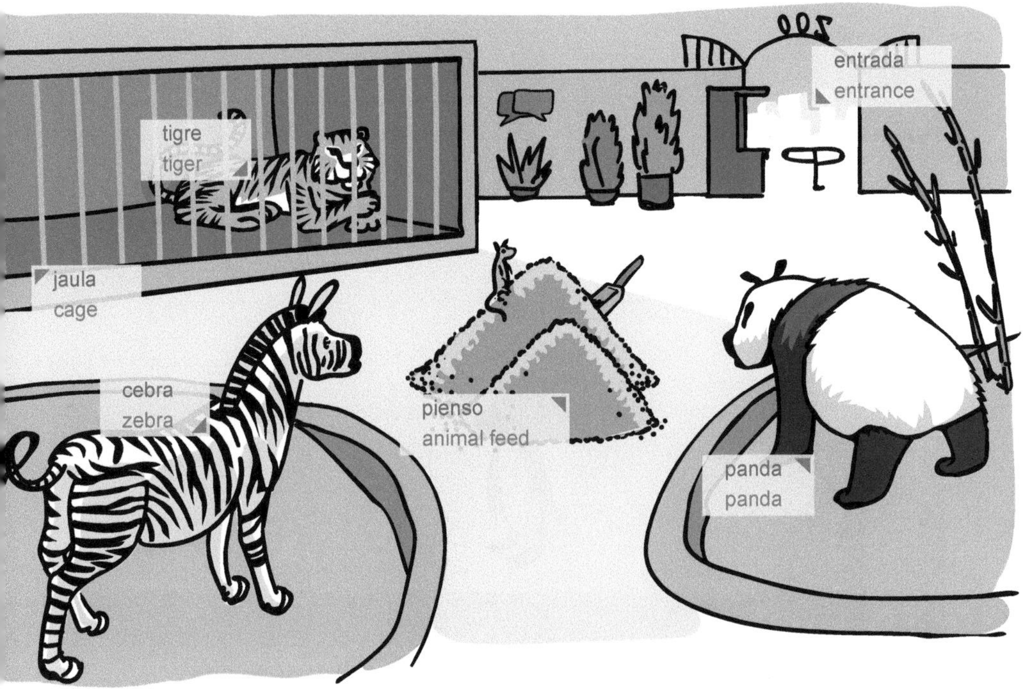

entrada
entrance

tigre
tiger

jaula
cage

cebra
zebra

pienso
animal feed

panda
panda

animales
animals

elefante
elephant

canguro
kangaroo

rinoceronte
rhino

gorila
gorilla

oso
bear

camello

camel

avestruz

ostrich

león

lion

mono

monkey

flamingo

flamingo

loro

parrot

oso polar

polar bear

pingüino

penguin

tiburón

shark

pavo real

peacock

serpiente

snake

cocodrilo

crocodile

guardián de zoológico

zookeeper

foca

seal

jaguar

jaguar

zoo - zoo

poni
pony

leopardo
leopard

hipopótamo
hippo

jirafa
giraffe

águila
eagle

jabalí
boar

pescado
fish

tortuga
turtle

morsa
walrus

zorro
fox

gacela
gazelle

fútbol americano
American football

ciclismo
cycling

tenis
tennis

baloncesto
basketball

natación
swimming

hockey sobre hielo
ice hockey

boxeo
boxing

fútbol

soccer

bádminton

badminton

atletismo

athletics

balonmano

handball

esquí

skiing

polo

polo

actividades
activities

saltar
jump
reír
laugh
abrazar
hug
caminar
walk
cantar
sing
soñar
dream
rezar
pray
besar
kiss

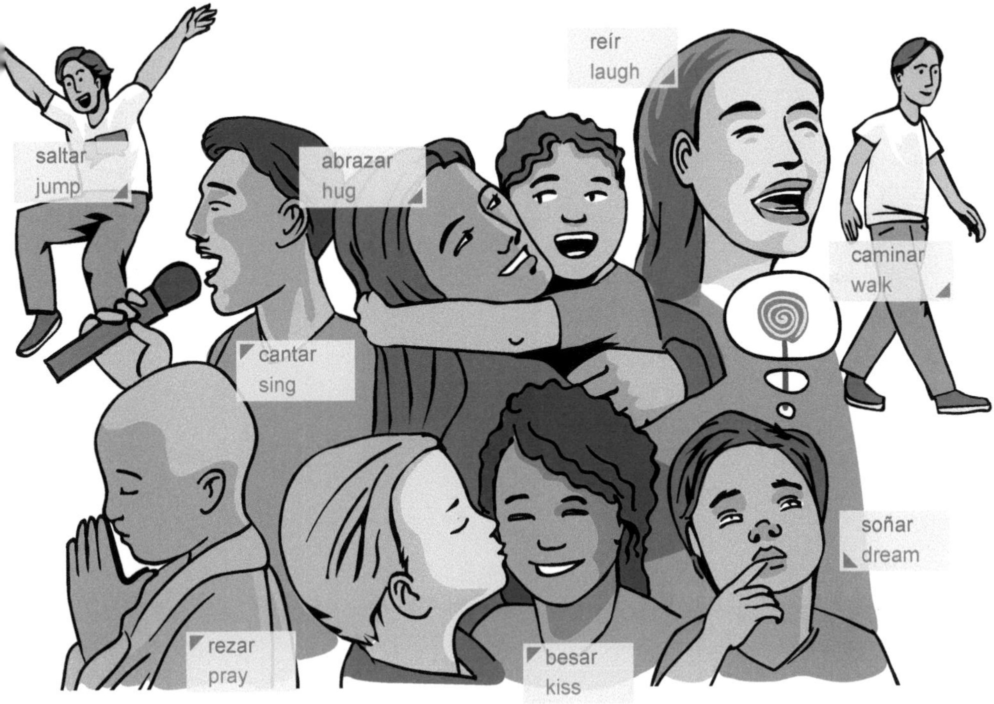

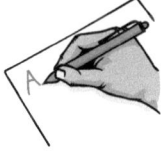

escribir

write

dibujar

draw

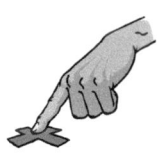

mostrar

show

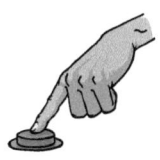

empujar

push

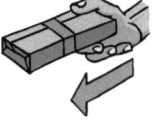

dar

give

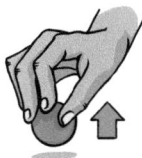

tomar

take

tener

have

hacer

do

ser

be

estar de pie

stand

correr

run

tirar

pull

tirar

throw

caer

fall

yacer

lie

esperar

wait

llevar

carry

estar sentado

sit

vestirse

get dressed

dormir

sleep

despertar

wake up

mirar

look at

llorar

cry

acariciar

stroke

peinar

comb

hablar

talk

entender

understand

preguntar

ask

escuchar

listen

beber

drink

comer

eat

ordenar

tidy up

amar

love

cocinar

cook

conducir

drive

volar

fly

navegar

sail

calcular

calculate

leer

read

aprender

learn

trabajar

work

casarse

marry

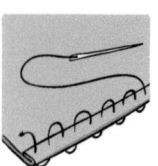

coser

sew

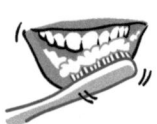

cepillarse los dientes

brush teeth

matar

kill

fumar

smoke

enviar

send

familia
family

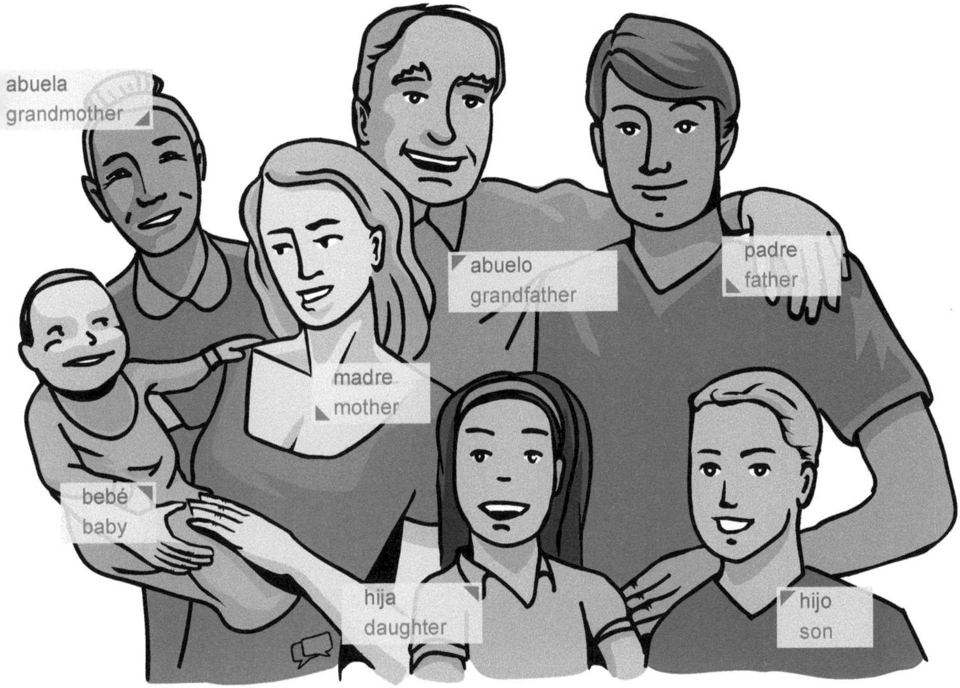
abuela
grandmother
abuelo
grandfather
padre
father
madre
mother
bebé
baby
hija
daughter
hijo
son

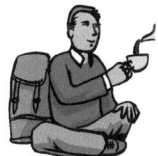

invitado

guest

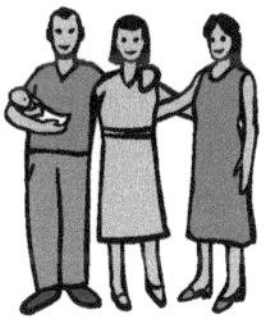

tía

aunt

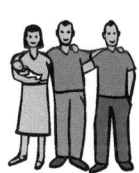

tío

uncle

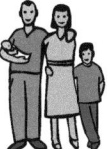

hermano

brother

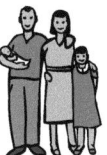

hermana

sister

cuerpo
body

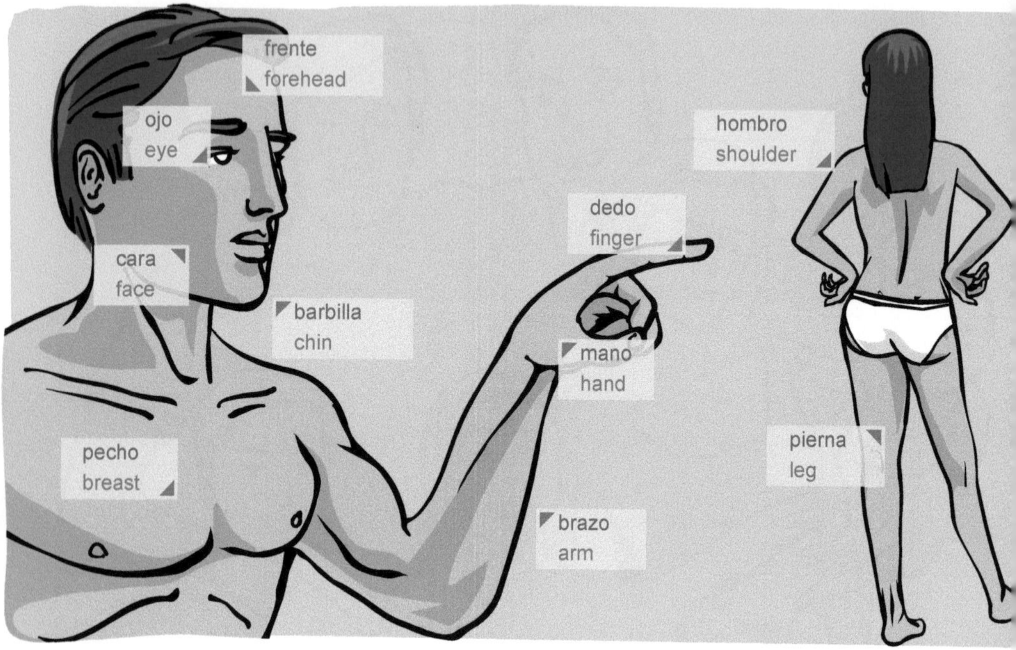

frente
forehead

ojo
eye

hombro
shoulder

dedo
finger

cara
face

barbilla
chin

mano
hand

pecho
breast

pierna
leg

brazo
arm

bebé
baby

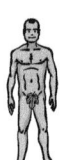

hombre
man

mujer
woman

chica
girl

chico
boy

cabeza
head

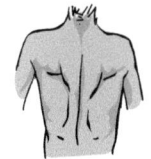

espalda

back

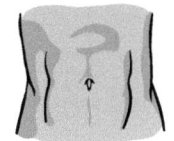

vientre

belly

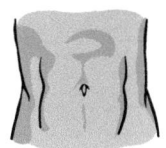

ombligo

navel

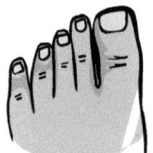

dedo del pie

toe

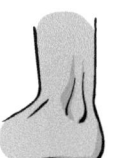

talón

heel

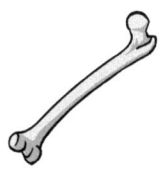

hueso

bone

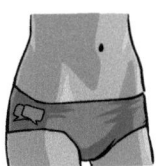

cadera

hip

rodilla

knee

codo

elbow

nariz

nose

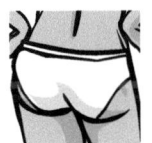

trasero

buttocks

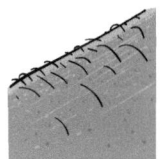

piel

skin

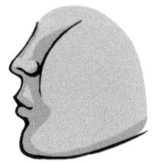

mejilla

cheek

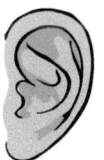

oído

ear

labio

lip

cuerpo - body

boca

mouth

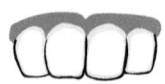

diente

tooth

lengua

tongue

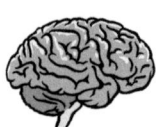

cerebro

brain

corazón

heart

músculo

muscle

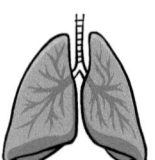

pulmón

lung

hígado

liver

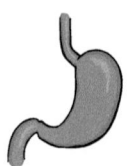

estómago

stomach

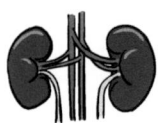

riñones

kidneys

sexo

sex

condón

condom

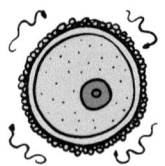

ovario

ovum

semen

semen

embarazo

pregnancy

cuerpo - body

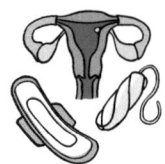

menstruación

menstruation

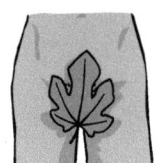

vagina

vagina

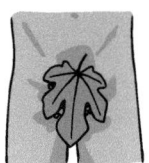

pene

penis

ceja

eyebrow

pelo

hair

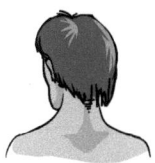

cuello

neck

hospital
hospital

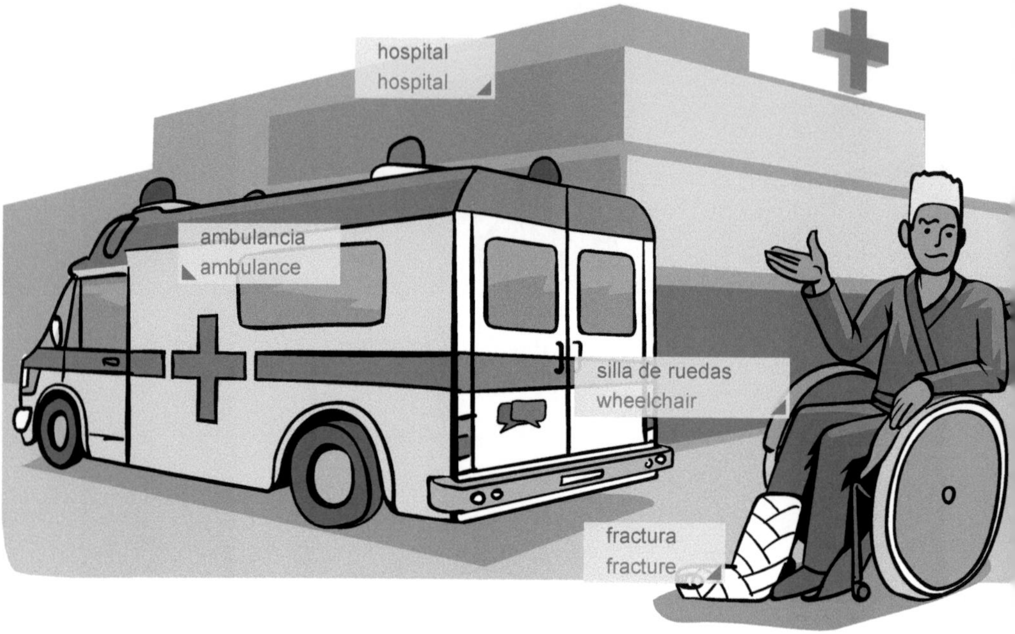

hospital
hospital
ambulancia
ambulance
silla de ruedas
wheelchair
fractura
fracture

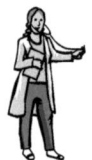

médico

doctor

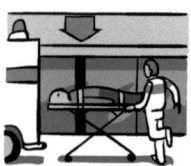

sala de urgencias

emergency room

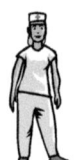

enfermera

nurse

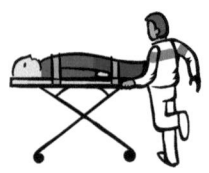

urgencia

emergency

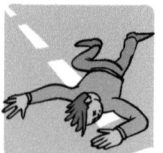

inconsciente

unconscious

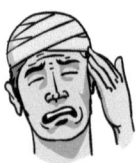

dolor

pain

lesión

injury

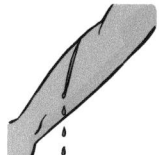

hemorragia

bleeding

infarto

heart attack

ictus

stroke

alergia

allergy

tos

cough

fiebre

fever

gripe

flu

diarrea

diarrhea

dolor de cabeza

headache

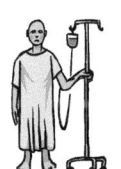

cáncer

cancer

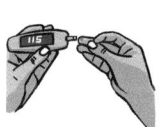

diabetes

diabetes

cirujano

surgeon

bisturí

scalpel

operación

operation

TAC

CT

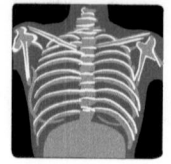

rayos x

x-ray

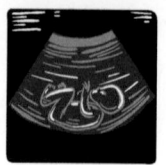

ultrasonido

ultrasound

mascarilla

face mask

enfermedad

disease

sala de espera

waiting room

muleta

crutch

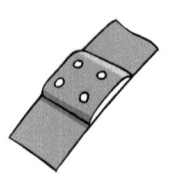

tirita

plaster

venda

bandage

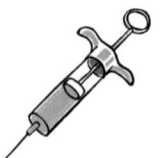

inyección

injection

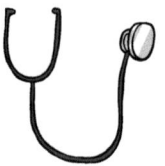

estetoscopio

stethoscope

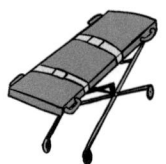

camilla

stretcher

termómetro

clinical thermometer

nacimiento

birth

sobrepeso

overweight

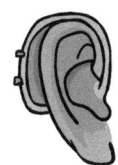

audífono

hearing aid

desinfectante

disinfectant

infección

infection

virus

virus

VIH / SIDA

HIV / AIDS

medicina

medicine

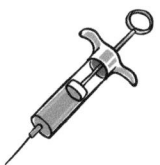

vacunación

vaccination

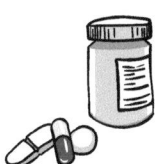

tabletas

tablets

pastilla

pill

llamada de urgencia

emergency call

tensiómetro

blood pressure monitor

enfermo / sano

ill / healthy

hospital - hospital

¡Socorro!

Help!

alarma

alarm

asalto

assault

ataque

attack

peligro

danger

salida de emergencia

emergency exit

¡Fuego!

Fire!

extintor de incendios

fire extinguisher

accidente

accident

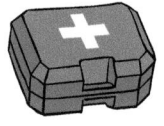

botiquín de primeros auxilios

first-aid kit

SOS

SOS

policía

police

Europa

Europe

Norteamérica

North America

Sudamérica

South America

África

Africa

Asia

Asia

Australia

Australia

Atlántico

Atlantic

Pacífico

Pacific

Océano Índico

Indian Ocean

Océano Antártico

Antarctic Ocean

Océano Ártico

Arctic Ocean

polo norte

North pole

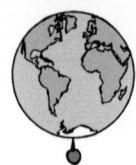

polo sur

South pole

Antártida

Antarctica

tierra

earth

tierra

land

mar

sea

isla

island

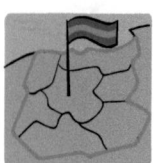

nación

nation

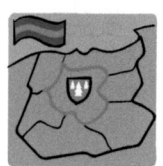

estado

state

esfera

clock face

manecilla de las horas

hour hand

minutero

minute hand

segundero

second hand

¿Qué hora es?

What time is it?

día

day

tiempo

time

ahora

now

reloj digital

digital watch

minuto

minute

hora

hour

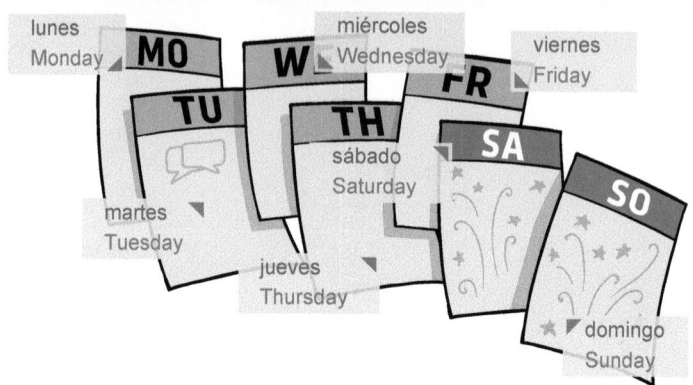

lunes — Monday **MO**
martes — Tuesday **TU**
miércoles — Wednesday **W**
jueves — Thursday **TH**
viernes — Friday **FR**
sábado — Saturday **SA**
domingo — Sunday **SO**

ayer

yesterday

hoy

today

mañana

tomorrow

mañana

morning

mediodía

noon

tarde

evening

MO	TU	WE	TH	FR	SA	SU
1	2	3	4	5	6	7
8	9	10	11	12	13	14
15	16	17	18	19	20	21
22	23	24	25	26	27	28
29	30	31	1	2	3	4

días laborables

workdays

MO	TU	WE	TH	FR	SA	SU
1	2	3	4	5	6	7
8	9	10	11	12	13	14
15	16	17	18	19	20	21
22	23	24	25	26	27	28
29	30	31	1	2	3	4

fin de semana

weekend

año

year

lluvia
rain
arcoíris
rainbow
nieve
snow
viento
wind
primavera
spring
otoño
fall
verano
summer
invierno
winter

4.APRIL 11°
5.APRIL 4°
6.APRIL 13°
7.APRIL 8°
8.APRIL 10°

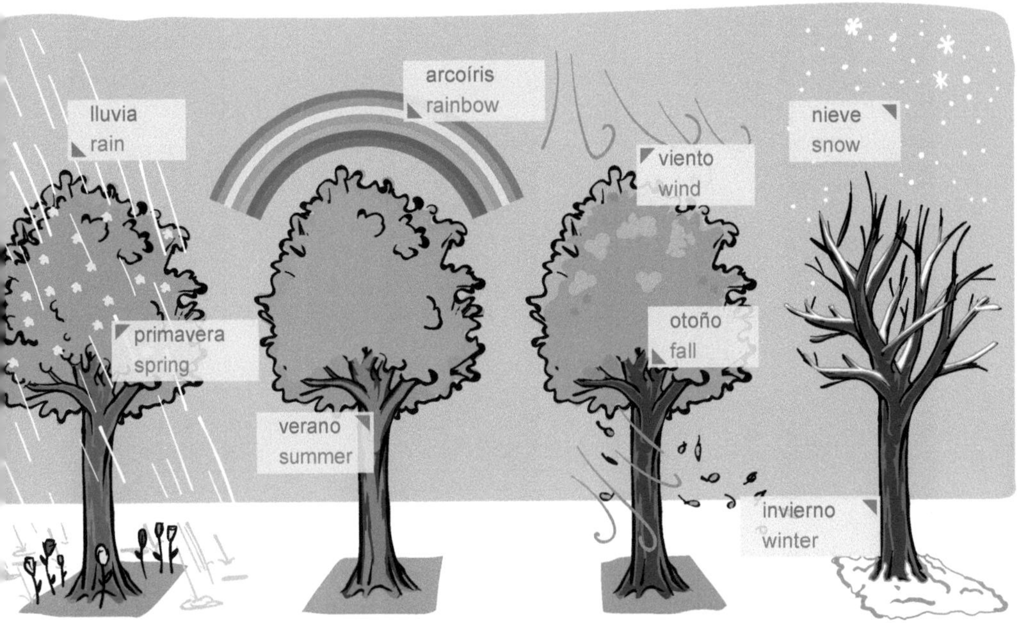

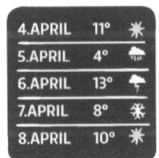

pronóstico del tiempo

weather forecast

F C
120 40
90 30
60 20
30 10
0 0
-30 -10
-20

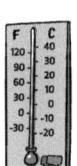

termómetro

thermometer

sol

sunshine

nube

cloud

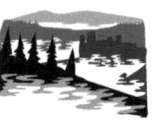

niebla

fog

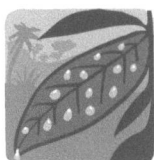

humedad

humidity

rayo

lightning

trueno

thunder

tormenta

storm

granizo

hail

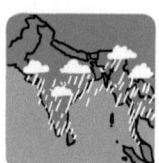

monzón

monsoon

inundación

flood

hielo

ice

enero

January

febrero

February

marzo

March

abril

April

mayo

May

junio

June

julio

July

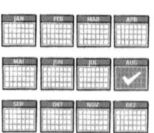

agosto

August

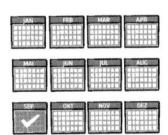

septiembre

September

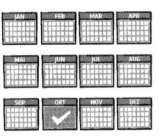

octubre

October

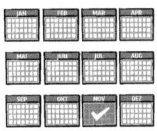

noviembre

November

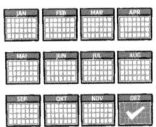

diciembre

December

formas
shapes

círculo

circle

cuadrado

square

rectángulo

rectangle

triángulo

triangle

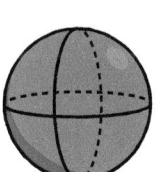

esfera

sphere

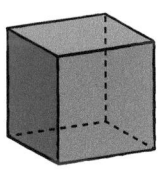

cubo

cube

blanco

white

amarillo

yellow

anaranjado

orange

rosa

pink

rojo

red

morado

purple

azul

blue

verde

green

marrón

brown

gris

gray

negro

black

mucho / poco

a lot / a little

enojado / tranquilo

angry / calm

bonito / feo

beautiful / ugly

principio / fin

beginning / end

grande / pequeño

big / small

claro / oscuro

bright / dark

hermano / hermana

brother / sister

limpio / sucio

clean / dirty

completo / incompleto

complete / incomplete

día / noche

day / night

muerto / vivo

dead / alive

ancho / estrecho

wide / narrow

comestible / no comestible

edible / inedible

malo / amable

evil / kind

entusiasmado / aburrido

excited / bored

gordo / delgado

fat / thin

primero / último

first / last

amigo / enemigo

friend / enemy

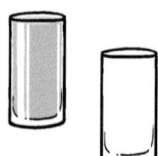

lleno / vacío

full / empty

duro / blando

hard / soft

pesado / ligero

heavy / light

hambre / sed

hunger / thirst

enfermo / sano

ill / healthy

ilegal / legal

illegal / legal

inteligente / tonto

intelligent / stupid

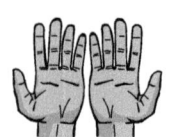

izquierda / derecha

left / right

cerca / lejos

near / far

nueva / usado

new / used

nada / algo

nothing / something

viejo / joven

old / young

encendido / apagado

on / off

abierto / cerrado

open / closed

silencioso / ruidoso

quiet / loud

rico / pobre

rich / poor

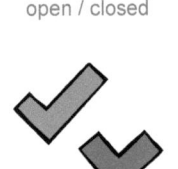

correcto / incorrecto

right / wrong

áspero / suave

rough / smooth

triste / contento

sad / happy

corto / largo

short / long

lento / rápido

slow / fast

húmedo / seco

wet / dry

cálido / frío

warm / cool

guerra / paz

war / peace

0

cero

zero

1

uno

one

2

dos

two

3

tres

three

4

cuatro

four

5

cinco

five

6

seis

six

7

siete

seven

8

ocho

eight

9

nueve

nine

10

diez

ten

11

once

eleven

12

doce
twelve

13

trece
thirteen

14

catorce
fourteen

15

quince
fifteen

16

dieciséis
sixteen

17

diecisiete
seventeen

18

dieciocho
eighteen

19

diecinueve
nineteen

20

veinte
twenty

100

cien
hundred

1.000

mil
thousand

1.000.000

millón
million

números - numbers

inglés

English

inglés americano

American English

chino mandarín

Chinese Mandarin

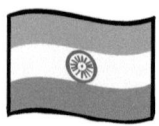

hindi

Hindi

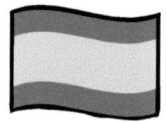

español

Spanish

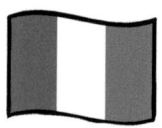

francés

French

árabe

Arabic

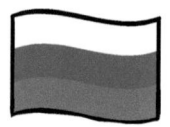

ruso

Russian

portugués

Portuguese

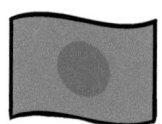

bengalí

Bengali

alemán

German

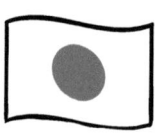

japonés

Japanese

yo

I

tú

you

él / ella / ello

he / she / it

nosotros/as

we

vosotros/as

you

ellos/as

they

¿quién?

who?

¿qué?

what?

¿cómo?

how?

¿dónde?

where?

¿cuándo?

when?

nombre

name

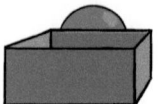

detrás

behind

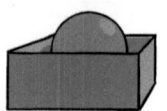

en

in

delante de

in front of

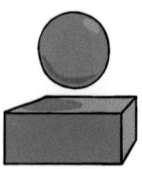

por encima de

over

sobre

on

debajo de

under

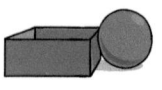

junto a

beside

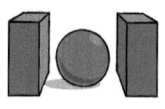

entre

between

lugar

place

.